STEAL MY
SECRETS

STEAL MY

SECRETS

A 1-DAY DIY GUIDE TO A KILLER RESUME

PROFESSIONAL RESUME WRITER

Marcie Wilmot

This publication is designed to provide accurate and authoritative information in regard to the subject matter covered. It is sold with the understanding that neither the author nor the publisher is engaged in rendering legal, investment, accounting, or other professional services. While the publisher and author have used their best efforts in preparing this book, they make no representations or warranties with respect to the accuracy or completeness of the contents of this book and specifically disclaim any implied warranties of merchantability or fitness for a particular purpose. No warranty may be created or extended by sales representatives or written sales materials. The advice and strategies contained herein may not be suitable for your situation. You should consult with a professional when appropriate. Neither the publisher nor the author shall be liable for any loss of profit or any other commercial damages, including but not limited to special, incidental, consequential, personal, or other damages.

Printed in the United States of America.

Visit the author's website at www.copyhawk.com.

Book cover by Neha Rasheed.

ISBN: 979-8-9890638-1-9 (paperback)

First Edition: August 2023

Contents

Introduction

Chances are good you're reading this book because you want to know how to create a resume that will land you a job. Am I right? Yes! And I'm so excited you chose this book because the purpose of it is to do just that: teach you how to build a highly effective and professional resume in just eight simple steps.

After multiple years of successfully designing, constructing, and revamping resumes for clients in numerous industries, I can assure you that this is very doable. Don't be intimidated! Over time, I have developed and refined a process that quickly and easily produces resumes that get results … and now I'm going to tell you all about it so you can do it yourself.

Now, don't be misguided. When I say "quickly," it doesn't mean that you'll be able to put together a resume in five minutes flat. To be realistic, it's something you can finish in a day – likely within just a few hours – if you follow the steps outlined in this book. You will have to put in some time and effort, but in doing so, will save yourself hundreds of dollars that would otherwise be spent on hiring a professional. You'll also significantly increase your odds of being contacted for an interview.

So why trust me? Because the resumes I create for job seekers get them noticed. They stand out among all the others. Having worked in both an HR and recruiter capacity, I know what it's like to post a job ad and end up with literally hundreds of resumes in my inbox. Honestly, after a while, they all blended together. But every once in a while, an awesome resume would appear on my screen, and I'd think, *Wow. This person has it together. Let's schedule* them *for an interview.*

Keep reading to learn how to create a resume that looks professional and polished, one that catches the attention of the folks who matter. Go ahead – open up a brand-new Microsoft Word document right now and get started on the eight steps I've outlined in this book, beginning with Chapter One. In less than a day, you'll have a finished resume that will impress employers and, with any luck, help you land your dream job.

Wishing you all the best –

Marcie Wilmot
Owner of CopyHawk.com
Resume Coach, SEO Writer & Editor

Chapter One

Gather Your Information

Let's start at the very beginning. Before you can do anything else, you'll need to compile all the information necessary to build an accurate and impactful resume. What does this involve exactly? It's not complicated and shouldn't take long, but you really can't skip this step.

If you do, you'll be taking several giant risks: that your resume won't 1) consist of anything meaningful, 2) make it past ATS (applicant tracking system) barriers and into the hands of recruiters and HR folks, or 3) appeal to your target audience.

So don't ignore this important first step! Spend some time right now compiling these items:

- *Your existing resume* (if you have one)

- *The information you'll need for your new resume* (if you don't already have an existing one) – At a minimum, list your **current and past jobs** (i.e., job titles, company names, company locations, start/end dates) and **education** (i.e., degrees/certifications, university/program names, graduation dates, and notable accomplishments). In addition, write down the details related to any relevant **technical and soft skills**, **volunteer experience**, **publications**, and/or **awards** that you have.

- *Some target job descriptions* – Find at least two job ads that appeal to you. Ideally, they should be for roles that you are truly interested in.

Now let's briefly talk about why you need the above information. First, if you have a resume – even one that's outdated or not overly impressive – it simplifies the entire process because you can refer to it for the basics (dates, titles, names) as you create your new one. If you don't, it's not a problem, but in this case, you'll need to list all of your job and education details somewhere so you can refer to them as you create your new resume.

Finally, it's extremely helpful to have a few target job ads to reference as you build your new resume so you can tailor the language properly and increase your odds of beating ATS barriers. Mirroring the key terms and phrases you see repeated in the target job descriptions will make your resume less generic and more impactful. Recruiters and HR folks will believe you have the experience, qualities, and skills they are seeking in a candidate.

Note: This doesn't mean you should copy a job description (or full sentences from one) word-for-word into your resume. It *does* mean, however, that you should look for words and phrases mentioned more than once (those that also apply to you and your skillset) and sprinkle them throughout your resume in meaningful ways.

These keywords might be qualities you possess, like being *collaborative, technically savvy, data-driven, proactive, passionate, flexible,* or *analytical.* They might also describe job duties (for example, *oversees reporting, mentors junior staff, creates engaging content, builds relationships,* or *develops marketing campaign assets*). Other times, it might be advantageous to include some industry jargon or acronyms from the job ads (*SEO, FIFO, CSS,* or *HMO,* anyone?) in your resume.

Remember, the goal is to make yourself look like you're the perfect fit for the role and the company. If the language in your resume reflects the language in the employer's job ad, they'll be more apt to think this might be the case. So read through several job ads that interest you, note any keyword repetition either manually or using an AI tool, and then incorporate the ones that apply to you into your resume.

And so, we conclude the first step in this easy-to-follow process of building an amazingly powerful resume. Begin by compiling the information you'll need (i.e., your existing resume or a list of your education/work information and at least two target job descriptions) and acknowledging the importance of tailoring the language in your resume to the job(s) you want.

Now it's time to move on to the next step: constructing your resume's framework.

Chapter Two

Construct the Framework

Here's a tip: you need to think about both the language *and* the visual appearance of your resume as you build it – equally. They both matter.

If your resume is filled with lots of incredibly written bullets that accurately convey all your capabilities but looks disorganized and unattractive, it'll probably get overlooked. On the other hand, if your resume is stylish and striking but filled with meaningless fluff, no one will take it seriously.

You need to nail *both* the content *and* the formatting of your resume to impress employers.

This step focuses on the layout of your resume, which, if done correctly, will lead to it looking professional, neat, and visually balanced. Let's break it down:

Page Margins

You're going to need plenty of space to say everything you want to say. Go to the Layout menu at the top of your Microsoft Office screen. Click on Margins and select the Narrow option. This will set all the margins of your document (top, bottom, left, and right) to 0.5 inches each. Perfect. Time to move on.

Page Border

Next, go to the Design menu and click on Page Borders. On the Page Border tab within the box that opens, select Box and ½ pt. width. Make sure to apply the border to the whole document. Now, having a border is optional, so you can choose not to add this element, but doing so will give an air of professionalism to your resume.

Tables

Now that you have your page margins and border in place, it's time to create some tables to add structure and organization to your resume. Go to the Insert menu, click on Table, and select two boxes down and two across (a 2x2 box). The box should automatically extend across the full length of the page (if it doesn't, drag it wider until it does). Then fill in the company name, location, job title, and start/end dates of your current employment, like below.

Company Name	City, State
Job Title	Start Date – End Date

To make your information pop, italicize the company name and bold your job title. Also, align the location and start/end dates with the right side of the table. If your company's name is a long one, you might need to drag the middle vertical table divider over a bit to compensate for that. Finally, highlight your table and select No Border so it looks like the example below.

Company Name   City, State
Job Title   Start Date – End Date

Then you can simply copy and paste the table you've created however many times you need (depending on the number of jobs you're including on your resume), and fill each of them in with the correct details. *Just make sure to hit the enter key a few times below each table before pasting another one so you end up with several separate tables and not one long one.* Later, you'll add bullets in these spaces.

A final comment here: Some people dislike tables and/or claim that they make it harder for applicant tracking systems (ATS) to read resumes. In my experience, tables don't interfere with this. However, if this is a concern of yours, it is possible to create this simultaneous left and right alignment appearance by using the Paragraph tab settings in Word instead of a table.

Font Type and Size

While there is some leeway when it comes to which font you should use on your resume, it's best to choose one that isn't distracting. In other words, *don't use this one* or this one.

Instead, stick with a standard font that is easy to read. And no, this doesn't mean you *must* use Times New Roman (although it's always a safe bet). You can go traditional or modern, sans-serif or serif – it's up to you – just don't pick anything too crazy.

Here are some common resume fonts:

Calibri (my favorite and the font used in this book)
Times New Roman (as mentioned above)
Arial
Avenir Next
Book Antiqua
Cambria
Garamond
Georgia
Helvetica
Palatino Linotype
Tahoma

Any of the fonts listed above will keep your resume looking sophisticated. Go with a font that suits you but doesn't overwhelm or confuse your reader, and you'll be good. Beyond that, only use black and keep your font size between 10 and 12 points. Twelve points is typically recommended by resume experts, but you might need to go slightly smaller to fit in all of your desired text.

Resume Length

Finally, let's not forget to answer the burning question on everyone's mind. **How long should your resume be?**

The quick answer is 1-2 pages. If you go longer than two pages, you run the very real risk of turning off the recruiter or HR person before they've even read your name. Too many pages will scare them away!

It might also give them the impression that you are overqualified for the job and/or old (ageism exists).

To decide between one or two pages, use these very easy guidelines:

- If you have less than 10 years of experience, keep your resume to one page.
- If you have over 10 years of experience, keep it to two pages max. One page also works if you're able to condense everything, while still keeping all your text easy on the eyes.

Now you know how to set up your resume's basic framework. Let's quickly summarize:

- Adjust your page margins to 0.5 inches.
- Add a simple page border.
- Use tables (or Paragraph tab settings) to add structure.
- Choose a font that is simple and legible.
- Keep your font black and 10-12 points in size.
- Make your resume a one-pager unless you have over 10 years of experience – then it's two pages at the most. Don't go longer than two!

Not too bad, right? To make things even easier as you continue to work on your resume, go to the View menu, select Zoom, and change it to 150% so you can really see everything on your screen, including the smallest of details.

Now let's discuss the header of your resume and how to make this section really pop.

Chapter Three

Create a Prominent Header

The purpose of a resume is to sell yourself and show all you have to offer to a potential employer. But what good is it to do that if the recruiter or HR person doesn't know how to get in touch with you to move forward in the hiring process? This is why you need a noticeable header at the top of your resume that clearly displays your name and contact information.

The good news is that this part of your resume is incredibly simple to create. Here is an example of how you'll want it to look:

YOUR NAME

City, State 00000 • (000) 000-0000 • youremail@address.com • linkedin.com/in/yourlinkedinurl

Name

It can be fun to pick the font for your name because it's acceptable to choose one that's a bit more exotic. Feel free to let your personality shine through, although, of course, you want it to be easy to read, and if you're in a more traditional field, you probably don't want to pick one that's too out there. The font used above for YOUR NAME is Calisto MT.

It's also suggested that you bold your name and make it big (the example above is 28 points). Additionally, it's a great idea to use all caps to differentiate it from the other text on your resume. To do this, highlight your name, right-click, and choose Font. In the Effects section on the Font tab, select All Caps, and then hit OK to save this change.

Don't forget to include any relevant credentials after your name, like specialized degrees and doctorates, if this applies to you. Some examples include Ph.D., MSN, MBA, and RN.

Line

To make a line under your name, simply press the enter key after it and type --- (three hyphens) on the following line. Press enter again, and the hyphens will automatically turn into the thin line you see above.

Contact Information

Next is your contact information, which at a very minimum should include your phone number and email address. Some folks also put their home address (this is generally advisable unless you're applying to jobs that are remote or out of state) and social media profiles, especially LinkedIn because it is a professional platform. It's also possible to include relevant blog or portfolio URLs here if you like.

Two quick tips: 1) Use an email address in your header that looks professional but isn't a work email, in addition to being one you check frequently. 2) When it comes to your home address, it's perfectly acceptable to put just your city, state, and zip code if you prefer since the chances of a hiring person contacting you via snail mail these days is practically zilch.

To mimic the header above, use Calibri (sized 10-12 points) and • symbols to separate your contact information.

To put bullets (•) in your header, click on the Insert menu at the top of your Word screen and then Symbol on the far right. If you don't see a bullet listed there, click on More Symbols... and select (normal text) in the Font box and General Punctuation in the Subset box on the Symbols tab. Select the bullet and hit Insert.

Once you have one bullet in your document, you can copy and paste it wherever you need. Alternatively, you can set up a shortcut key for this symbol.

Finally, be aware that if you choose to include your LinkedIn profile URL on your header (a good idea if you have one set up with multiple connections), you should shorten it first so it looks nice and fits in your header. To do this, edit your custom URL within your profile settings on LinkedIn. It's generally best to change your URL to your first and last name or something similar.

Pretty easy, right? Let's review:

- Choose a font that resonates with you and make your name large and bold at the top of your resume so everyone knows it's yours!
- Insert a line to separate your name and contact information.
- Add your phone number and email address (at a minimum) so the employer knows how to reach you.
- If you choose to include your LinkedIn profile URL, first simplify and shorten it.

Now it's time to tackle what's probably the hardest part of a resume: writing your work history bullets. But don't worry! The next chapter will walk you through exactly what you need to do to be successful. Keep reading to learn how to conquer this challenge.

Chapter Four

Highlight Your Professional Experience

We've arrived at the section of your resume that will likely require the most time and effort to complete. Here you will create bullets that detail your current and past job responsibilities and accomplishments. It's critical to produce bullets that are clear, accurate, and impactful because most recruiters and HR folks will focus intently on this part of your resume.

Remember the tables you created in Chapter Two that you filled in with your employment information? Now it's time to put bullets below them. Here is an example of how this will look:

Company Name   City, State
Job Title   Start Date – End Date

- Write a powerful sentence here describing your job duties and measurable achievements.
- Write a powerful sentence here describing your job duties and measurable achievements.
- Write a powerful sentence here describing your job duties and measurable achievements.
- Write a powerful sentence here describing your job duties and measurable achievements.

Note that **your bullets should be placed *outside* your tables.** If you put them *inside* a table, it will screw up your formatting. To better understand this, see below with the table borders turned on.

Company Name	City, State
Job Title	Start Date – End Date

- Write a powerful sentence here describing your job duties and measurable achievements.
- Write a powerful sentence here describing your job duties and measurable achievements.

- Write a powerful sentence here describing your job duties and measurable achievements.
- Write a powerful sentence here describing your job duties and measurable achievements.

See? You *don't* want to do this:

Company Name	City, State
Job Title	Start Date – End Date
<ul><li>Write a powerful sentence here describing your job duties and measurable achievements.</li><li>Write a powerful sentence here describing your job duties and measurable achievements.</li><li>Write a powerful sentence here describing your job duties and measurable achievements.</li><li>Write a powerful sentence here describing your job duties and measurable achievements.</li></ul>	

Because if you put your bullets inside your table, your resume won't look right at all:

Company Name   City, State
Job Title   Start Date – End Date

- Write a powerful sentence here describing your job duties and measurable achievements.
- Write a powerful sentence here describing your job duties and measurable achievements.
- Write a powerful sentence here describing your job duties and measurable achievements.

- Write a powerful sentence here describing your job duties and measurable achievements.

Make sense? Okay! Now let's talk about how to write your bullets. Below are several tips and suggestions to help you put your best foot forward.

Tip #1: Start Your Bullets with Strong Action Verbs

One of the easiest ways to differentiate your resume from others is to use powerful action verbs at the beginning of your bullets. Why? Because most people start their bullets with boring and overused words like performed, worked with, responsible for, and assisted – sometimes using them repeatedly.

But the words you use matter a lot! So instead of starting your bullets with weak, sad verbs that will impress no one, use awesome ones like:

accelerated	demonstrated	fostered	orchestrated
accomplished	designed	gained	overhauled
achieved	developed	generated	presented
advised	established	improved	produced
contributed	exceeded	increased	saved
coordinated	expanded	initiated	sold
cultivated	facilitated	maximized	streamlined
delivered	forged	optimized	supervised

Try not to repeat your action verbs so the recruiter doesn't see, for example, *developed* or *supervised* 20 times on your resume. If you're stuck, type the word + definition into Google (e.g., *developed definition*) and check out all the synonyms that come up (in this case, some of them include *grew, evolved, expanded, initiated, instituted, originated, invented, established,* and *generated*). See? There are so many other great verbs you can use instead of repeating the same few a million times. **It's easy to avoid repetition if you use synonyms.**

To hit the *strong action verb* point home, check out some examples below.

(Weak) Bullets with Weak Action Verbs:

- Participated in meetings with the regional manager and sales team.
- Assisted in the daily maintenance of several online databases.
- Worked in the head office as an accountant.
- Had the responsibility to record and make entries in the firm's internal system.
- Worked cross-functionally with internal partners and teams.

(Strong) Bullets with Strong Action Verbs:

- Forged and nurtured meaningful relationships with clients, colleagues, and management.
- Championed the safety of thousands by providing strong leadership and strict oversight.
- Mitigated risks by conducting security assessments and applying procedural improvements.
- Delivered responsive and customized IT support for numerous companies across the U.S.
- Supervised junior auditors and reviewed their work for precision and compliance issues.

See the difference?

Finally, *don't begin any bullets with adverbs, adjectives, or nouns.* Instead, using strong verbs will add consistency and an action-oriented mindset to your resume.

> ➢ As a side note, if you're not a fan of writing, you might want to consider using an **AI tool** to write some (or all) of your bullets for you. There's absolutely nothing wrong with doing this! Just be sure that you read through all of them and modify them as needed to ensure accuracy and relevancy.

Tip #2: Highlight Achievements and Use Lots of Numbers

To bring your resume to the next level, do more than just generically list the job duties you've had in the past. While a lot of your bullets will naturally describe your various responsibilities, keep in mind that HR folks are more interested in the contributions you've made.

In other words, **how have your actions benefited your former employers?** Did you identify issues and improve processes? Did you close a significant deal or build a team from scratch? Before writing your bullets, brainstorm what you've accomplished in all the roles you've held.

Then when you write about all your impressive feats, **use numbers** in these bullets whenever you can. Why? Because they visually stand out, making it easier for people to see the exact, quantifiable impact you made in previous jobs. Their thinking will then likely go something like *if she did that for them, then she'll probably do the same for me.*

What kinds of numbers should you include in your bullets? Metrics and key performance indicators (KPIs) that measure success. Below are some examples, and you can probably think of others as well.

- clients you acquired or retained
- income from these acquired/retained clients
- sales revenue increases
- cost savings
- overtime cost reductions
- quotas/targets you have exceeded
- team size and/or number of staffers you managed
- staff retention statistics
- audit findings
- budget amounts
- donations you collected
- website traffic increases
- user engagement increases
- subscriptions you sold or renewed
- student test scores
- response times
- customer ratings

As you can see, there are lots of options. Pick the ones that apply to you and your field, and then incorporate them into your bullets. Putting this extra effort in now will pay off in dividends in the future.

Tip #3: Reference Target Job Ads for Bullet Ideas

Plagiarism is never acceptable, but there's really no need for you to reinvent the wheel either. When you're writing your bullets, refer to the target job ads you've identified for inspiration.

Right off the bat, as we talked about earlier, you should be using keywords and phrases in your bullets that you see repeated in your target job ads to boost your chances of outsmarting applicant-tracking software.

Beyond that, your primary goal should be to show potential employers that your skill set and experience match what they seek. And since what they want from a candidate is spelled out in their job ad, it's an obvious place to draw ideas from when you're writing your bullets.

For example, if your dream employer states in their job ad that they want to hire someone who is adept at building relationships, you can create a bullet highlighting your achievements and ability in this area. *Wherever your skills, personality traits, and experience overlap with what the employer wants, write bullets to reflect that.*

Tip #4: Create More Bullets for Recent Jobs Than Older Ones

You might be wondering how many bullets you need to write. Good question! Here are some general guidelines that will help you figure this out:

- If you have over 10 years of experience, aim for about 25 bullets across two pages.
- If you have less than 10 years of experience, aim for 10 to 15 bullets on one page.

You should craft more bullets for your recent roles than your older ones since employers will focus more intently on your latest experience. Here's a breakdown of the number of bullets you should write per job:

- Last five years of experience: 10-15 bullets
- Next five years of experience: 5-10 bullets
- Next five years of experience: 5 bullets total
- Beyond 15 years ago: no bullets

If you want to mention work history that is older than 15 years ago, consider including it in a centered, italicized sentence underneath the rest, like this:

Prior Experience: Assistant General Manager, United Parcel Service (May 1998 – Jan 2000)

The main takeaway here is to spend more time writing bullets for your recent jobs, especially your present one (or last one). Older experience still matters to employers but less since they know it's probably no longer fresh in your mind. Emphasize the newer skills and experience you've gained by creating more bullets for your recent roles.

Tip #5: Write Your Bullets so They Fit the Width of the Page

Another way to ensure that your resume ends up head and shoulders above the competition is to create bullets that fit the width of your resume. Most people don't think twice about doing this, but if you do, you'll end up with a visually striking resume that outshines the rest. Let's take another look at the example from above:

(Weak) Bullets with Weak Action Verbs:

- Participated in meetings with the regional manager and sales team.
- Assisted in the daily maintenance of several online databases.
- Worked in the head office as an accountant.
- Had the responsibility to record and make entries in the firm's internal system.
- Worked cross-functionally with internal partners and teams.

(Strong) Bullets with Strong Action Verbs:

- Forged and nurtured meaningful relationships with clients, colleagues, and management.
- Championed the safety of thousands by providing strong leadership and strict oversight.
- Mitigated risks by conducting security assessments and applying procedural improvements.
- Delivered responsive and customized IT support for numerous companies across the U.S.
- Supervised junior auditors and reviewed their work for precision and compliance issues.

Not only are the verbs on the bottom list more powerful than the ones above, but do you notice how these bullets go across the entire page without falling onto the next line? On the other hand, the ones on the top list vary in length, drawing the eye to their asymmetry.

If you can keep your sentences a similar length that extends across the entire page, the result will be a resume that looks neat, professional, and attractive. Most readers won't even realize that this is the reason your resume looks so much more polished than the other ones. ***It's a secret trick that really works!***

Admittedly, it can be a bit of a challenge to get all your sentences the right length. This is another instance when using synonyms comes in handy (refer to tip #1). Sometimes it's just a matter of swapping out a longer word for a shorter one to fit your bullet on one line. But while it might take some additional time to produce bullets of similar lengths, it's worth it because it'll differentiate your resume from most of the others out there.

So there you have it! To recap:

- Start your bullets with powerful action verbs.
- Highlight contributions that benefited past employers.
- Throw in plenty of numerals.

- Tailor your language to your target job(s).
- Emphasize your newer skills and experience.
- Write sentences that fill the whole page.

This is by far the most time-consuming and challenging part of creating a resume, but your bullets will make or break your resume. So power through it (using AI to help if you need) and get it done!

Now let's talk about your education ...

Chapter Five

Add Your Education and Technical Skills

By now you should have the header, work history, and basic layout of your resume all set. Not too much more and you'll be all done! (Let's just say that the light is at the end of the tunnel.)

This chapter covers how to add your education and technical skills to your resume. Rest assured that this part of the process is pretty simple. So let's go ahead and dive into the details, in addition to answering some questions you might have:

Where should I put my education?

If you have **recently graduated or have little real-world work experience**, it's a good idea to put your education at the top of your resume (underneath your header, of course, but above your professional experience).

On the other hand, if you **have more than a year or two of work experience**, it's more appropriate to put this section at the bottom of your document.

There are some other instances when you might put this section at the top of your resume:

- If you are switching industries and want to highlight a relevant degree or certification.
- If your degree is from a particularly prestigious university (oooh, go you!)

➤ Most people, however, will list their education and technical skills at the bottom of their resume. If you're at all unsure, it's recommended that you do this as well.

Should I include my GPA?

It's generally only a good idea to include your GPA on your resume if it's a 3.5 or higher and you have little work experience. Most people don't include their GPA on their resume, so if this is stressing you out at all, just leave it off.

If you haven't been in the workforce long (let's say under three years), it's fine to list your GPA along with your degree. In fact, doing so can help assure a potential employer that you earned decent grades in college and are indeed relatively bright. Since you likely don't have much work experience at this stage, a good GPA will serve to bolster your overall credentials.

Note that if you want to sound fancier, you can also choose to write cum laude ($\geq$ 3.0 GPA and a class rank of 75% or higher) or magna cum laude ($\geq$ 3.4 GPA and a class rank of 85% or higher).

Should I include the date I graduated?

You can, but you can leave it off just as easily too. So how do you decide?

If you're older and trying to avoid ageism (while technically illegal, we all know it exists), it's best to list your degree without a graduation date. While any recruiter or HR person worth their salt will still likely figure out approximately how old you are, it's generally wise not to smack them in the face with your age if you can help it. Make them work for it. Encourage them to focus on what you have to offer before considering your age.

And if you're not concerned about age discrimination or more recently graduated? Then feel free to include your graduation date. Ultimately, it's optional and completely up to you!

Here's an example of how your education and technical skills section might look:

EDUCATION & TECHNICAL SKILLS

New York University • **Bachelor of Science Degree in Business** • New York, NY

HubSpot • Microsoft Office (Excel, PowerPoint, Word, Outlook) • Monday.com • Google Workspace • Zoom

See how simple it is? There's no need for it to be complicated.

If you are comfortable using lots of computer programs, include two or three lines of them. If you have additional degrees or certifications, include them too.

Keep reading for some more tips:

Tip #1: Include ALL of Your Relevant Education

Most of us immediately think of college degrees when we get to this part of a resume. But what if you don't have a college degree? Or what if you've taken a bunch of online courses, earned some certifications, or received lots of training in your last role?

Here's the truth: all employers honestly care about (at least 95% of the time) is that you've spent time learning about some of the topics related to the job at hand. Yes, there are going to be some companies that demand a specific degree from a certain type of school.

But in many cases, there's a lot of flexibility here.

Aim to show the reader that you have some knowledge in the areas related to the position. Most importantly, make sure that whatever you list is relevant to the role at hand.

So if you're applying for an associate brand manager role, for example, list all the marketing-related courses you've taken via LinkedIn and Google in addition to any official degrees you have. If you received sales training in your last position that seems helpful, include that too. Meanwhile, downplay or leave off the animal grooming certification you got 10 years ago before you discovered your passion for marketing. Get the idea?

Here are some examples of what is often included in this section:

- university degree(s) – school name, degree, field of study, location (optional), graduation date (optional), GPA (optional)
- honors you've received
- educational achievements (e.g., dean's list)
- study abroad programs
- relevant coursework
- extracurricular activities
- online courses
- certifications
- professional training

If you attended college but never graduated, simply list the information (university name, field of study, location) without naming a degree or graduation date. If you'll be graduating at some point, include your expected graduation date.

Tip #2: Put Your Highest Degree First

If you have multiple degrees (awesome!), cite the most prestigious one at the top and then list the rest in reverse chronological order (the most recent to the oldest).

Tip #3: Leave Off Any High School Information

To be blunt, no one cares that you graduated high school unless you are still in college and trying to score an internship. If you have a college degree, there's absolutely no need to include anything about high school on your resume.

Tip #4: Highlight Your Technical Skills in This Section Too

As mentioned above, this is also where you should list the software you know how to use. **Be sure to look at your target job ad and include any programs on your resume that apply to you.** Doing so will earn you bonus points with the employer, plus any ATS program they might use.

Any relevant memberships or achievements can also be listed in this area of your resume, although you might want to put them under a new section title – something along the lines of "Affiliations & Memberships" or "Professional Achievements."

In general, this section of a resume is pretty straightforward. Throw some information about your degree on there, along with any relevant computer programs you know how to use – end of story.

However, there are a lot of questions that can pop up around what qualifies as education and so on. Hopefully, if you had any, they're all clearly answered now.

It's time to move on to step six … showing an employer that you have the right personality and all the soft and hard skills they need. Let's get right to it!

Chapter Six

Showcase Your Relevant Skills and Qualities

An employer wants assurance that you're going to fit into the company culture – and have all the necessary know-how to do the job. We're at the point in the process where you prove that.

How? By highlighting your relevant soft and hard skills, strengths, and personality traits. While this is achieved somewhat in the other language throughout your resume, you'll have an edge over the others if you create a section that's entirely dedicated to these attributes – and put it right at the top of your resume.

Here's an example of how this section might look:

Group Counseling • Conflict Resolution • DMH Documentation • Crisis Interventions • Substance Abuse Case Review & Management • Medication Compliance • Drug Screenings • Client Assessments Biopsychosocial Frameworks • Telemedicine • Community Outreach • Family/Caregiver Support

Exceptional Communicator • Motivated • Collaborative • Discreet • Proactive • Personable • Bilingual

Here's another example:

Revenue Generation • Sales/Marketing • Onboarding/Training • Staff Retention • Vendor Management Strategic Planning • Budgeting • Negotiation • Team Building • Recruiting/Hiring • Patient Care

Expert Communicator • Energetic • Collaborative • Resourceful • Proactive • Personable • Data-Driven

Beyond giving the reader an easy way to get an idea of all the skills you possess and who you are as a person, this section will help your resume beat ATS barriers. Those programs look for specific keywords – this section provides them, thereby helping to ensure your resume makes it through and isn't simply discarded.

Things to Keep in Mind:

- Only add skills that are relevant to the job you want. If you're running out of room, prioritize them and include the most meaningful ones.

- To get a good idea of the skills that matter to the employer you're targeting, read the job ad thoroughly. Note the skills and personality traits mentioned (especially repetitively) and incorporate any applicable ones into your resume.

- Read through your work bullets to find skills to add. For example, if you have a bullet on your resume that talks about overseeing a budget, include budgeting as a skill.

- Always include communication as one of your skills. In the examples above, you'll see *exceptional communicator* and *expert communicator* listed. Other descriptive terms you can use before communicator are *excellent* or *strong*.

Examples of Qualities You Might Include:

analytical	decisive	honest	resourceful
bilingual	discreet	motivated	self-starter
collaborative	driven	organized	strategic
creative	entrepreneurial	personable	tech-savvy
data-driven	energetic	proactive	versatile

Sound good? Okay, great! In the next chapter, we'll add an impactful and expressive title above these skills to round out the top portion of your resume. We're moving right along — you're almost done!

Chapter Seven

Formulate a Powerful Title

Ready to take your resume to the next level?

Most people don't know about this step. They simply slap their work experience and degree on a sheet of paper and are done with it. THIS is the step that makes your resume different than nearly all the others out there.

It will make your resume memorable, unique, and compelling.

And it's less than a sentence long. You can do this, and if you do, your resume is really going to stand out.

Let's start with some examples:

STRATEGIC SOLUTIONS-DRIVEN MARKETING EXPERT

Passionate and Experienced Leader Who Drives Innovation, Revenue Growth and Operational Excellence

INNOVATIVE & DRIVEN NETWORK ENGINEER

Solutions-Oriented Technical Expert Leverages Deep Functional Knowledge to Drive Operational Success
Passionate and Highly Experienced Problem Solver Seeks Challenging Sales Engineer Role

COLLABORATIVE SOLUTIONS-DRIVEN MANAGER

Experienced and Knowledgeable Leader Who Builds Teams and Drives Operational Success
Proactive Problem Solver Who Identifies Creative Solutions and Develops Strategies to Foster Engagement

CAPABLE & CLIENT-FOCUSED PROJECT MANAGER

Experienced Leader and Problem Solver Who Expertly Delivers Projects On Time and Within Budget
Driven Self-Starter and Entrepreneur Who Possesses Superior Knowledge of the Trades

STRATEGIC PUBLIC SAFETY & SECURITY DIRECTOR

Highly Accomplished Corporate Executive Targeting a President/VP Role in the Gaming Industry

DYNAMIC FINE DINING GENERAL MANAGER

Experienced and Knowledgeable Leader Who Drives Operational and Financial Success

Combined with Chapter Six's skills and qualities, your resume header will ultimately look something like this (remember, your name and contact information go above this):

STRATEGIC MARKETING AGENCY PRESIDENT

Accomplished Senior Leader Who Drives Profitability, Innovation and Operational Excellence
Entrepreneurial Visionary with Extensive Leadership Experience Pursuing a C-Level Management Role

Strategic Planning • People Management • Operations • Negotiation • KPIs/Metrics • Business Development
Budgeting • Financial Management • Marketing Strategy & Methods • Process Optimization • SEO
Consultative Selling • Recruiting • E-Commerce • Sales Enablement • Brand Development/Management

Exceptional Communicator • Decisive • Honest • Collaborative • Adaptable • Resilient • Results-Driven

Following this structure lends to a powerful resume that clearly conveys your aspirations, what you've achieved, and what you have to offer. Done right, it carries a significant impact.

How to Create Your Title

So how do you come up with the perfect title? Honestly, this part can be a little tough and might take some time. That's okay. Let's break it down:

1) **Pick an adjective or two** that describes both who you are and the qualities you think the employer wants for this role. Try not to choose adjectives mentioned elsewhere in your resume's top section (avoid sounding repetitive).

2) **Choose a job title** that accurately conveys who you are professionally. You might simply use the job title that you currently have (or last held). Or you can come up with a brand-new title that portrays both your career history and aspirations in one fell swoop.

3) Put the adjective(s) (e.g., Consultative, Results-Driven) in front of your desired job title (e.g., Sales Director) and you'll have a title for your new resume: Consultative Results-Driven Sales Director. Sometimes it's necessary to play around with the words for a few minutes until you come up with a title that fully conveys what you want to express.

4) While optional, including a sentence or two (bolded and italicized) below your title that further explains who you are, what you're trying to achieve, and/or what you have to offer will help ensure that this section really packs a punch.

➢ **If you're struggling here, try consulting an AI tool**, which can pump out multiple title options for you to consider. Even if they only serve as inspiration, sometimes this is an easier place to start than staring at a blank page.

The key to this part of your resume is to discern exactly what you want to convey to the person looking at your resume. *You want to literally capture the essence of who you are and what you're trying to achieve and distill it into just a few easy-to-understand words.*

And don't be bashful! If you're like every other job hunter out there, you have lots to offer – you might just need to realize this. Put serious thought into what your strengths are and what you're capable of and then use the top space on your resume to relay this to others. Believe in yourself.

And with that said, we've already arrived at the last chapter in this guidebook! Congrats on making it this far. If all went as planned, your new resume should be nearly complete at this point. Now let's just finish up by making sure it is perfectly polished and professional-looking ...

Chapter Eight

Make Final Adjustments and Proofread

Now that you've carefully followed all the steps above, it's time to put it all together. Here's what your resume may very well look like now (albeit with different language):

YOUR NAME

Your Address • (000) 000-0000 • email@address.com • linkedin.com/in/xxxxxxxxx

COLLABORATIVE SOLUTIONS-DRIVEN MANAGER

Experienced and Knowledgeable Leader Who Builds Teams and Drives Operational Success
Proactive Problem Solver Who Identifies Creative Solutions and Develops Strategies to Foster Engagement

Strategic Planning • Program Implementation • Talent Development • Resource Allocation • Process Optimization
Budgeting • Performance Management • Policies & Procedures • Public Relations • Event Management • PTO Administration
Operations • Interviewing & Recruitment • Crisis Intervention • Scheduling • Advertising • Employee Relations • Compliance
Personable • Exceptional Communicator • Innovative Thinker • Quick Learner • Active Listener • Bilingual (English/Spanish)

--- PROFESSIONAL HISTORY ---

Company Name   City, State
Job Title   Oct 2018 – Present

- Oversee the facilitation and implementation of community programs for a thriving non-profit that serves 35k+ students.
- Partner with school leadership teams, the community, families, and agencies to initiate and establish beneficial services.
- Collaborate with various stakeholders to identify services that support school initiatives and champion these programs.
- Coordinate valuable community resources (tutoring, arts, recreation, primary health) to further district-wide initiatives.
- Engage the public in strategic partnerships that meet critical needs and support student achievement in over 40 schools.
- Maximize the value of provided services and programs through development, promotion, and subsequent monitoring.
- Mentor and teach new employees about the non-profit's policies and procedures; support their onboarding experience.
- Facilitate event logistics and publicity (public relations, advertising, collateral material design/production/distribution).
- Lead the implementation of measures to track all spending and ensure adherence to budgets; solicit in-kind donations.
- Stay abreast of accounting trends, tools, and best practices to maintain the organization's first-class financial standing.

Company Name   City, State
Job Title   Mar 2016 – Oct 2018

- Governed the daily youth care operations for a charity that provides community mental and behavioral health services.
- Managed 70 youth care workers as a grounds supervisor and 10 in-house; ensured consistent attendance/performance.
- Cultivated trusting and respectful relationships with employees, upper management, peers, and community members.
- Trained new hires on organizational policies and procedures; kept staffers and clients informed of all relevant guidelines.
- Utilized HR software program, ADP, to efficiently manage employee timesheets and paid time off (vacations; sick time).
- Interviewed applicants following a standardized scoring guide of behavioral questions and led monthly training groups.
- Played an integral role in crisis intervention, emergency/conflict situations, and the physical management of residents.
- Supported the development of numerous treatment programs, therapeutic interventions, and proper living standards.
- Created a safe, empowering, productive, and equitable environment with an open culture for employees and residents.

Company Name   City, State
Job Title   Jul 2015 – Mar 2016

- Consulted with patients, families, physicians, nurses, and colleagues to arrange and implement high-quality patient care.
- Met with 15+ clients on a weekly basis to review the status of their cases and provided direct translations as needed.
- Forged meaningful professional relationships with federal service providers, coworkers, management, and customers.
- Conducted in-depth assessments and planning sessions to ensure patients received quick, respectful, and attentive care.
- Documented and maintained comprehensive clinical records; managed discharge details upon completion of treatment.

--- EDUCATION & TECHNICAL SKILLS ---

Society for Human Resource Management (SHRM) • **SHRM Certified Professional Credential (SHRM-CP)** • 2022
SHRM-CP earners are recognized for their ability to effectively perform HR duties in an operational capacity.
Name of University • **Bachelor of Arts Degree in Psychology** • 2016
ADP • Microsoft Office (Excel, Word, Outlook) • Google Workspace • Zoom

---

Just a few more things to consider as we wrap things up:

Use Paragraph Settings to Control the Spacing

One of the biggest challenges during this process typically arises when we need to fit everything on one page (or two if you're further into your career). This may require you to eliminate some less-important bullets. In addition, you'll likely need to use **Microsoft Word's Paragraph Settings** to manipulate the spacing throughout your resume so everything fits exactly the way you want.

For example, say you have two lines of text showing up on a second page. In this case, you'll need to condense everything so it all fits on one page. You may be able to do this by removing some of the space around certain sentences on your resume.

This might be as easy as changing the line spacing for all your bullets to Single under Paragraph Settings. Or you might need to get rid of some of the space before your name at the top of your resume to bring everything else up higher on the page (to do this, highlight your name, go to Paragraph Settings under the Home tab, and adjust the Before Spacing on the Indents and Spacing tab).

If necessary, you can also highlight headers (or other sentences) throughout your resume and remove or add space around them. You'll probably be surprised at how much control Paragraph Settings gives you when it comes to the spacing on your resume – it's so helpful!

Just try to make sure that 1) you keep the spacing consistent throughout the document and 2) you utilize white space as much as possible to ensure your resume easy to read.

Use a Special Header on the Second Page

If your resume ends up being two pages in length, consider adding a modified header at the top of the second page that looks similar to this:

While you won't want the elaborate header you created for the top of your resume in this spot, it's advisable to have your name and basic contact information there. A basic header, like the one above, works perfectly.

Use AI and Human Proofreaders to Check Everything

Finally, the last (but definitely not least) piece of advice: **proofread, proofread, proofread.**

Honestly, this really can't be emphasized enough. Details matter. It's absolutely crucial that your resume is impeccable so you impress your future employer. This means no typos, no grammar mistakes – essentially, no errors of any kind.

So don't hesitate to use AI-enhanced programs like Grammarly to check your resume. And ask several people you trust (friends, family, mentors, etc.,) to look it over and provide feedback.

No matter what you do, make sure your resume is as perfect as it can be before sending it anywhere. After all, it's a reflection of you and the best way you can show others why they should hire you.

And there you have it: eight DIY steps to create a killer (polished, professional, stand-out) resume in only a day.

In most cases, your first impression on a potential employer is your resume, and we all know how critical it is to nail that. Fortunately, we can spend all the time in the world – and get help from whomever we want – as we strive to make our resume powerful, visually compelling, relevant, accurate, and persuasive. Add in the secret tips and tricks revealed in this book (as well as several rounds of proofreading!), and you'll be well on your way to impressing anyone who looks at your resume.

So don't doubt yourself or give up. You can do this — really anyone can, especially with the help of AI these days. Follow the eight steps outlined in this guidebook, and before you know it, you'll have a winning resume in hand that will score you interviews and ultimately land you a great job.

If any questions or concerns come up, feel free to visit CopyHawk.com for additional help. Wishing you all the best and lots of luck always!

About the Author

Marcie Wilmot has revamped and built from scratch hundreds of resumes for clients since founding her company, CopyHawk, in 2019. Beginning as a freelancer on Upwork, she has gradually developed a process that enables her to consistently create resumes that delight her customers and impress employers.

Marcie thoroughly enjoys using her passion for writing to highlight all of her clients' strengths, skills, and achievements on paper, many times literally transforming the way they see themselves. The resulting boost in confidence has helped many of them take the leap – ditching micromanager bosses, moving up the ladder, switching industries, and more.

She's hopeful and excited about the idea of this book giving readers the ability to craft amazing resumes themselves without having to fork over lots of money to professional resume writers.

Beyond resume work, Marcie is a prolific SEO blog writer, editor (of books, documents, AI-generated content, etc.,), and content manager. She has a Bachelor of Science degree in Marketing from Clemson University and is a volunteer coach for Girls on the Run.

Married with two daughters, she is a lover of music, nature, animals (especially dogs), writing, and good food.

To read more of her writing, follow Marcie on Medium (@copyhawk) and view her blog and portfolio at copyhawk.com. To connect with her, you can find her on LinkedIn (in/marciewilmot), Facebook (CopyHawk), and X (@copyhawk_com).

Made in the USA
Monee, IL
03 October 2023

43892275R00026